EⅡR

Poulet Reine Elizabeth

Coronation Chicken

By Maria Masington

This edition published by
Parnilis Media
P.O. Box 1461
Media, Pennsylvania 19063

ISBN: 978-1-954895-26-3

Contact the author at mariam@lutz-engr.com or the publisher at matt@parnilis.com

CONTENTS

Dedication
for R.P.L.III & D.S.L.

ACKNOWLEDGEMENTS

The following have been previously published:

"Praying with Mark Twain," *Rockvale Review*, 2023

"Homer's Warning to His Son," *The Raven's Perch*, 2023

"Coronation Chicken," Big City Lit, 2022

"Taking on Water," *The Raven's Perch*, 2023

"Custody," *The Raven's Perch*, 2022

"The Orbit of Venus de Milo's Marriage," *The Raven's Perch*, 2023

"Lucky Number," *Moonstone Press Anthology*, 2022

"And deliver us from evil," by *Fridas of Barcelona* and *The Blue House of Surrealist Fridas*, 2022

Chicken Game

Don't look at this
chicken

GAME OVER

Coronation Chicken

PART 1

Mockingbirds
    after "The Hurting Kind" by Ada Limón

I have always been too loud, a desperate voice
        from a long line of noise.

We learn from the best, repeat curses, recite
        prayers.

From a faraway village, my great-grandmother's
        old wives' tale:

put a few drops of your own urine in your ears
        when they hurt.

I understand. It is painful to hear myself talk.
        Our family trills

whatever tune it takes to be heard. No whisper-
        down-the-lane

for us, we shout in streets. Our mountain women
        plead and hiss

at doctors who confuse lack of education
        with ignorance.

Wives bang fists on tables, scream the truth
        about cheating.

Sons are safe; priests know their mothers
        are mouths almighty.

My mouth is armed, my throat loaded with bullets
        from a long line of guns.

Quattro Nonne

Elizabeth, Theresa, Rosemarie, Paulina, my personal Rushmore. Larger-than-life faces carved in granite. Flawed, hard-core women, ancestral blood on bed sheets, in kitchen sinks, staining knuckles that delivered a mean left hook. Haloed through suffering, saints of the hardscrabble, mined from Calabrian mountains. They knew the answers to my questions, how to solve any problem. My friends adopted as family, pinches of oregano, plum tomatoes, squash flowers. Enemies became their targets, witches around our cauldron of Sunday gravy. Salts of the earth, I built my life on the backs of five-foot-nothing goddesses, Joan of Arcs, their scent of smoke and Jean Naté, bunched-up Kleenex. Big mouths painted Cherries in the Snow, quick tempers, five-and-dime wisdom. They taught me to fight, love, never accept *no*. When I am overwhelmed, I remember my mother's mother holding my face, saying, *my mother would be so proud of you.* I too will die exhausted.

Consigliere

One of the dons calls an emergency meeting.
We gather after A.A. and Weight Watchers,
from boardrooms and salons. Dented Subarus
and new Mercedes squeeze into her driveway.
Under cover of darkness, we use the backdoor
and don't knock.

Assembled around the kitchen table, coffee poured,
poundcake sliced, laptops charged so we can Google,
assess, plot. Thelmas and Louises, ride-or-dies,
original gangsters, vigilantes. Villagers who stormed
Frankenstein's castle, torches lit, pitchforks sharpened.

Through cancer, financial crises, abusive partners,
career changes, pain-in-the ass kids, depression,
social injustices, taking parents off life-support.
CEOs and homemakers alike, we change bandages,
bail water out of basements, do background checks
on sons-in-laws.

Because we choose to keep showing up
with picks and shovels, maps and headlamps—
we are the women who know
where the bodies are buried.

Teetertotter

On the playground a tall boy sat across from her.
As his seat quickly thunked to earth, she flew off,
crashed to cement and cried to Sister Gwen, bone
protruding from arm. Life is not fair, even, or equal
but in her case crisis and catastrophe pair, tie.

When it rains, it pours, not just cats, dogs, but capybaras,
Gila monsters. Twisted Noah's ark. The day she went home
to ask her parents for help getting sober, they opened the door,
and spat at her, *Good, you're here. We're getting divorced.*
The day she retired to caretake a tough mother, now a weepy
ball of unremembering, her dad stroked, but Good news!
Only his memory is affected.

During her lumpectomy, her kid got beaned with a baseball
and ambulanced to ICU at Children's Hospital. Cellphones
were not yet a thing. She started spotting an hour before her
grandmother died, bled through the funeral. Next day doctor
scraped out her dead baby.

She prays hard stuff will be uneven, stair-stepped so she can
focus on one drama at a time. Maybe breathe in between,
let her hair grow thick again, sleep through a night, hear a phone
ring without an apoplectic shrill that makes her heart race. Maybe
the nuns were right—God is punishing her. Nervous system
always on overload, constantly forcing ideas into her prefrontal
cortex, so the rational brain prevails.

Her Morton Salt girl yellow dress and shoes are muddied a spicy
mustard hue, huge umbrella blown inside out. The unfairness
of a balanced seesaw is she never gets thrown off, cannot crash,
say I am broken.

A String of Ponies on Chincoteague Island

As a kid, I grouped everything into families.
Mother ant and her offspring. Caterpillar sisters.
Groups of both are called armies. A bunch

of sharks, a shiver; parrots, pandemonium.
The horses here travel in family units, tawny
bodies on the dunes gently gallop side by side.

My own family was a tangle, twisted together
bed sheets in a clothes dryer, knotted
necklaces at the bottom of a jewelry box.

We dreadlocked into a matted mane
that we could not brush free. So we unbraided
and ran to different corners of the ring. We keep

our distance to survive but it's lonely. I watch
families on the beach, big clans posing for photo
shoots as casts of crabs scurry by. I fantasize

that in crisis we might unspool from our separate
bobbins and, for a split-second, weave together a
lifeline. No longer unraveling, but still tightly wound.

Prayer of a Practical Mother

I never taught my child to dream; we set attainable goals and plan how to achieve them. Women broken by disappointment produce children who never lose their heads in the clouds.

Our minds never wander to lottery wins, miracles, or happily-ever-after's. We hope for safety nets: affordable health care, the ability to make good decisions, for things to be "fine."

Star light, star bright, first star I see tonight

Down-to-earth people drive through the world with sunroofs shut, blocking out pollen, debris, carjackers, moon glow, sunlight, the sweet kiss of April air. And yet, bad seeps in.

Voice over Bluetooth, *it's 2inches long and malignant.* The other shoe, I'm constantly ready for, drops. Images of things 2 inches long rain down: a golf tee, a credit card, an egg, a pink eraser.

I wish I may, I wish I might

The 10 mile an hour driveway to the hospital entrance is flanked by blossoms of cherry, pear, crabapple. In gusty spring winds, I slide the sunroof open, allow delicate blush and ivory

petals to confetti my gray hair and the interior. I weep as they land gently, flower girls down the isle of fate. Pray the doctor is rested, my child is strong, never allow myself to hope for the best.

Get the wish I wish tonight.

Barbie Doll, 1977

She needed someone
more manly than poor
effeminate Ken, molded
hair, creamy skin.
So, the little girl stole her
brother's G.I. Joe, with the
rough beard, fatigues, and
weapon, to orchestrate
passionate make-out sessions
for the doll and her man.
Boy crazy, they said.
Boy crazy, so young.
Crazy they refused to see
what had happened to her
when she reenacted it
again, and again, and again.

Lucky Number

It's a hard knock life for us she hears, yet again—
her children are obsessed with *Annie.* They know
their mother is an orphan, who, not recalling
show tunes in foster care, hates this movie.

Four biological kids, who all look like her, icy
eyes, white-blond hair. *Make my bathroom shine*
they sing and dance, as she leans on the sink,
behind a locked door. Directions tremble in her

hands, mouth dry as she tries to spit in the tube.
Blocking out the toddler knocking, fighting over
popcorn, she shakes the vial for five seconds,
squeezes her eyes shut in hope. 23andme,

an opportunity, roll of the dice, to find a great
aunt or cousin match, not allowing the ultimate
fantasy of half-siblings or parents. *No one cares
for you a bit,* seeps in, as she imagines

a teenage boy, pimp, or enraged grandfather
skulking into the Trenton bus station, a moving,
mildewed rucksack dropped onto the floor outside
the ticket window, her umbilical cord still attached.

Custody

Therapist, mediator, judge,
I type each in my calendar

then walk, a quiet hour before our
kid swap at the attorney's office.

Each step, I wonder when we
began destroying each other.

The night your eyes slowly,
subtly started to wander?

The first time your voice
felt like nails in my head?

I trudge the acorned path, blue
sky suddenly shadows. Red-tailed

hawk, wide-winged, a gray squirrel
hanging like a grimace from its

talons, omnivore head and bristle
tail limp. I watch a second hawk

bullet in, trying to steal the catch
or kill the bird? In battle, the furred

body spins down, hitting the ground
with a solid thump. I am a reluctant

witness, like our child, but I have
power to turn away. Which one will

win in the end? The raptor who lost
its meal, or the aggressor? We both

logged miles in all the shoes:
killers, fighters, prey.

F.R.O.G.

My arm stretches toward him on puddled pavement,
bleach-white belly up, mouth hung open,

legs jutting to the sides under relentless sun.
I look for tire marks, a shoe print, but he is whole.

A pristine specimen, victim of last night's storm.
Frogs have lungs. Their skin absorbs oxygen under water

but if there is not enough, and no dry land to jump onto,
their lungs fill with water. Bloated little amphibian

drowned in his own element. The torrent swallowed him. I
sense flood in the gutters grow. Huge waves crash me down.

I scramble through darkness, break through the surface,
quickly gulp air, before the next curl of water crumbles me.

I give him a flowerbed funeral, gently lay him under
a butterfly bush, shout to the heavens, *Fully Rely On God!*

I pray to a god I don't understand. I hear the rumble
in my mind, see the swell moving closer, wait for it

to drag me under again. I hope some god remembers
I too have lungs and need dry land. I could easily drown.

Chicken Game

Don't look at this chicken

GAME OVER

Coronation Chicken

PART II

The Orbit of Venus de Milo's Marriage

She trusts no one, not even this man
who went around and around proving
himself again and again. She is cautious,
no arms to break her fall.

Worry takes her millions of miles away.
Terrified that her wedding band, like Saturn's
gold ring, is not what it seems, just a tangle
of rock, dust, and ice. Goddess of love, marble

heart that once beat and bled, hardened
by betrayal, gradually turned to stone.
Visible in her bare torso, chunks of flesh
stolen by past lovers, shaped by volcanic
rages, surface worn to a pearly hue.

Did she chisel off her own foot so she could not
run away this time? Keep herself from kicking him
off the pedestal where she placed him? She is his
morning and evening star, bright light, masterpiece.

Praying with Mark Twain
Go to Heaven for the climate, Hell for the company.
                                        Mark Twain

If we could have met in the last fiery years,
after Tom and Huck, later when
you lost your wife of decades,
buried children stolen by
meningitis, diphtheria, mental illness,
as miscarriage and divorce jaded me.

Self-destructing in young womanhood,
having burned every bridge I crossed.
Alone. You, no grandkids to tell your tales.
I'd have listened, near the end of your life
when they say you had volcanic rages and
fought depression with cigars and books.

Not to rehash the Mississippi Queen, Yale, or
Halley's Comet. No, we'd compare war
stories, connect over anger, injustice, neither
needing to apologize or make excuses,
a communion of regret and shame.

And then, after talking late into the scorching night,
I'd light two cigarettes in my mouth, pass one to you,
and in holy, smokey covenant, with *tobacco hearts*,
you'd assuage my resentment and say,

"Settle down, girl, remember:
Forgiveness is the fragrance
that the violet sheds
on the heel that has crushed it."
And I would respond, "Amen."

Taking On Water

I am not Monet's lily.

Not floating among shiny
lily pads or flowering pastels.
I am the rusty underside.
Claude Monet — I dare you.
Dive in, submerge yourself,
see a mother who has not bloomed,
glistened, slept for ten months.
Color me in murk,
paint me black.

I am not Ophelia.

Not young or noble yet I too
live grief. Mad from not knowing
where he is, drowning assuages terror.
But in water things clear. I am parent
first. Refuse to inhale, dig nails into silt,
push up, gasp through lakes mirror.
I scream
come home my boy.

I am not Virginia Woolf.

Everyday another stone shoves into
my pockets. Load me with rocks,
worst case scenarios. Label me
tragic, victim, survivor. I charge
into brackish silence. But as water
circles my neck, I unload
the sodden coat, trudge ashore in case
he needs me.

Parable of the Prodigal Daughter

I am a woman who has two daughters, the oldest vaporized
a decade ago. Her sister, just a little girl then, became
child-servant to our grief. So, when the text arrived
from a number we had never seen before, we rolled out
red carpet. My younger daughter begrudged this intimate
stranger nothing.

Fresh flowers in the tombed bedroom, new coat of paint,
old photos displayed. When my older girl dramatically
breezed in and announced, *Here I am, your prodigal child
has returned,* we threw our arms around her and kissed her,
automatically forgave, swept the past under faded carpet
and allowed our hearts to crack back open.

On our knees we thanked God, and my younger girl threw
a party. As the reunion unfolded, I began to revise the
Gospel according to Luke. When my older daughter
disappears again, I will proclaim, *You are always with me,
and everything I have is yours.*

Then I will get my gold rings from the safe deposit box,
place them on my younger daughter's fingers,
buy her sandals made from the best Italian leather,
iron the finest robes, ask my husband to go out back
and kill our fatted calf.

Coronation Chicken

The regal name, so important sounding, that I ordered
without reading the ingredients. It's basically chicken
salad. No pomp, no circumstance, just meat, apricots,
mayonnaise, served cold.

I felt the same letdown on what I was told would be
the happiest day of my life. Love, but no joy, just an
overwhelming sense of impending responsibility
to keep him safe and alive. The task seemed daunting at 25.

Queen Elizabeth was 25 when she took the throne, national
responsibility placed upon her head encased in a five-pound
crown of jewels. A gold trimmed cloak, the literal weight
of the world, draped around her stoic shoulders.

Holding my seven-pound baby, I felt the burden. The yoke
around my neck. I was chicken, sans fruit, sans dressing,
postpartum depression butchering my dried-up carcass.
Positive he'd be better off with another mother, scared

to bathe him, terrorized by his cry, I crumbled as he turned
his head away, weaning himself at five-weeks-old,
and behind the disappointment, relief.

Homer's Warning to His Son

I see her, all wave and curl along the shore.
I hear birdsong trill, inviting you to inhale

her scents of salt and sex and jasmine. Black
hair, green-eyed siren, wings spread wide.

She is id afire; do not breathe her smoke.
It is not her fault. Feathered mask

hides half woman, half vulture, all bait
and switch. Can't you see her hollow glare?

Perched on a mound of bones and teeth
and glasses of men who could not see red

flags through rosy lenses. She waits
to hold you down with polished talons,

use her painted beak to gut you like
a fish. I know. I too was once a lamb

beckoned to slaughter beach. But I listened to
my father, stuffed my ears with beeswax

so I could no longer hear. You are not special.
Believe me. I can guarantee how this story ends.

Let me tie you to the mast, young Ulysses,
tighten the ropes until you can safely row past.

... and deliver us from evil...

I float on my milky bed; bare feet splash white.
Under a canopy of Snowy Owl's wings, I twist in
madness and grief. Depressed waves threaten to drown me.

Frida Kahlo died at 47, Alejandra Pizarnik at 36. I am 25
and determined not to die. Bed of milk, Snowy Owl's
golden talons pull me to surface, let me gasp for air.

The Joker comes to my milky bed, begs me to be his bride,
united in suffering. Greasepaint lips electric against my neck,
white-gloved hand on the sweet small of my back.

I must refuse to take the Clown Prince's throne. I cannot wed
myself to a lifetime of his anguish, so golden talons pluck him up
and deliver him to another woman's nest.

Alejandra Pizarnik pours herself onto me. Whiskey-breath kiss,
she blows a jumble of high heeled words that sensuously tiptoe
up my neck but could accidently slit my throat.

She tries to convince me that she knows the way out, but I
cannot listen to her well-meaning distractions. Return to me
Father Owl, take Alejandra gently in your beak.

Deliver her to the beach of her homeland so she can bask
in sun and sea, where voices drown and hopelessness
crabwalks from her body and digs itself a sandy grave.

Return to me with Frida Kahlo in your gilded grips. Deliver her
to my bed, where I splash and thrash in milky sheets. I will beg
her to wring out my dishtowel body. Faded and fraying

where barbed sadness ripped my cotton reality. Ask her to connect
her bloody heart cord to mine. Let me rub rosed oil onto her bare feet.
She will float beside me, paint my grief and madness, feathered

brushes blending blues, reds, soft yellows, and greens.
I will gather my strength, face the pain, as Frida Kahlo
graciously weaves flowers into my sodden hair.

A Nod to Robert Frost and Bill Wilson Off Kamehameha Highway

Through a hole in a chain link fence, I step
onto a dusty path through banyan and fir, myna
bird chatter, jagged slag underfoot as walls of jade
rise and fall like breath from the ocean floor

to join a swarm of locals and tourists
gathered to experience forty-foot-high waves.
On this volcanic hill in Oahu, I lean against
an abandoned Machine Gunner pillbox
where twenty-year-old old men once fought.

My battle started decades ago when,
at a turning point, I found a hole in a fence
that would save my life if I were brave enough
to enter—knowing it would be lonely, difficult,
that there were *easier, softer* ways.

In musty church basements, day after hundreds
of thousands of days, veterans mapped out
how it works. Always tempted, I'd cry out
I can't go through with it, only to log another
twenty-four hours.

Palm trees arch their long necks to kiss the horizon.
Sunlit peacock colors swell and spill. I remain dry
above gusty lava tube spray, crashing majesty.

This too shall pass, but today I
Trudge the Road of Happy Destiny

and that has made all the difference.

Long Haulers

As dusk slowly cracks open, its hot yolk sun burns
the bay, floating an inch above the horizon, gilding

waves and sand. The world split by a thin dark strip of
land, half air, half water, copper star slipping from view.

A penny for your thoughts I say, but you just shake
your head. Have you no ideas, or are the thoughts

relentlessly rolling, one after another? Perhaps you fear
my two cents, differing opinion, disappointed tone.

No matter how carefully I measure my words, I know
I will misspeak, or you will misinterpret. *This is your*

new normal the doctor says. We are coated in fear, sand
sticking to legs and bare feet, battered, fried. We head

back up the beach in heavy silence, silhouettes on a
purple backdrop, maneuvering around driftwood,

rocks, cautious not to step on sharp and unrelenting
shards of clam, oyster, and eggshells.

UNFORGIVEN

The first bar I ever snuck into was Deer Park Tavern
where Edgar Allan Poe stumbled one night, exclaiming,
"A curse upon this place! All who enter shall have to return!"
Don't drop acid! Take it pass/fail! was written on the Ladies
Room wall. "Clever," I thought to my 16-year-old self,
"But why take anything pass/fail when you can knock it
out of the park?" When I grade my own paper, I get an A
because I mean well, but I misspeak, misstep, repent and repeat.
Chipped bricks pave my road to hell, one best intention at a time.
A Post-it on my mirror reads *hit a homerun today* meaning don't
do or say anything you'll regret. No matter how hard I try,
there are curve balls, fouls, hollers of "strike!" I pray I won't
need fake ID when I die. "Enter, you did your best." In reality,
I'll stand exhausted, while my Higher Power, who looks a lot like
Poe on a bender, takes red Sharpie and scrawls across my forehead.

Haiku of Mercy

violet sky
follows sunset, forgiveness
in a purple cloak

Please Drive my Urn over the Verrazano Bridge
in Worcester County, Maryland

She never collected horses, asked Santa for a pony, or read
Misty of Chincoteague. Horses made her sad. In kindergarten
her family went to Assateague where wild equine live without
metal shoes, hay, or vets, on a thin island between a bay and moods
of the Atlantic. She got a snow globe with a filly in it. She shook
it and prayed *Let the horses be safe. Make my parents stop fighting.*
Like beasts on hardscrabble land, she was trapped between people.

Now, midlife, she returns and falls in love with these animals.
Pregnant mares, bachelor bands, female-led harems of caramel,
chocolate, cream. Awed by deep hoof prints in sand, powerful
gallop up and down dunes, their freedom, tenacity through seasons
of icicles on their eyelashes, stinging insects, squalls, heat, nor'easter,
tourists in minivans. She sits on the beach, absorbs their powerful grace,

breathes their musk, listens as they munch scrub grass, rip it up
with their teeth, chew. They are connected, she and these ponies,
sink or swim, thriving in places that are inhospitable, but home.
She is the oldest person she knows whose parents are still alive.

Hers have not seen or spoken to each other in forty years, both still hostile,
ever-changing landscapes. One sucks her dry with windy bluster, the other
hides like a spooked colt. The island is her boundary, she tells them there is

no reception, to anchor one voice, quiet the second. She'll return home to
dozens of frantic texts from the first, then have to find the other, reel them
back in, convince herself that when they pass away, she'll have no regrets.

She tells her kids that when she dies, *please spread my ashes on Assateague.*
Shake me like a snow globe, she prays so I glisten on clear green bay, cling
to stallion legs and run free. Sprinkle me among wooly yellow heather, so
when the mare lies down, I can finally rest under a blanket of tawny velvet.

Chicken Game

Don't look at this
chicken

GAME OVER

Coronation Chicken

PART III

Fleeing the Beach House at 4:30 AM

I hoped to meditate
as apostrophes of dolphins
arch over waves and

speckled Lady crabs
dig in sugar sand.
But I walked here in rage

—over how I allowed her
to speak to me, her
unwillingness to take it back.

You could haunt a house
with that smirk. My part in it
is my inability to let it go.

I am blinded by anger. As a bitter
orange sun rises, I can't tell if I see
dolphins or sharks. A Ghost

crab, big as a Vidalia onion,
scratches over my sunburnt
feet. A Laughing gull screams.

Mother of the Bride: Self Portrait

I began drawing myself one-dimensional during pregnancy.
Foreseeing mistakes, inadequacy, sketched a good parent,
incessantly erased failure, blended colors to tone myself
down. My daughter, who hated the mess of fingerpaint,

is now a radiant bride, my son escorts me down the aisle.
Joyful illustration, yet all I see is Pollock-splatter of regret.
Therapists called; red flags overlooked. Later I command
the dancefloor as my family stares. Shed my jacket, Electric

Slide outside pen and ink boundaries, Cupid Shuffle from
Linear scribble right into "Uptown Funk," back to when
my brushes were paint-full. Summer mint, tangerine, patchouli
melded, blurred the canvas edge as I twirled. Smoke gently

rolled us back to tents, drums, paperback philosophies where
I loved their father on a mildewed sleeping bag. Around us
voices billowed, grew into "Scarlet Begonias." Then a size
zero twenty-something, living like a fleshy Rubens nude.

Now sixty, a size ten who whittled myself to a stick figure.
It is my fault they don't know I can dance, serve as muse,
masterpiece, neon waterfall on black velvet. Fear made me
a forgery, raising them with straight lines and pastel colors.

Today in church I vowed to be a Rothko.
I will no longer love my kids with anxiety
but embrace them in unfixed happiness,
reintroduce my mother-self: *Orange, Red, Yellow.*

40th Anniversary at Lake Ariel

Mourning Cloak butterflies startle
as I pace the yellow-yarrowed shore.
Cattails burst into seed, bass ripple
the surface, mockingbirds taunt me.

Focused on a thin strip of water
between the pines — I channel
Victorian women who waited
for their men to return home from
the sea. I watch for the tip of the
kayak to float him into view.

My husband: who refuses sunblock and vitamins, forgets his medication,
puts off taking his blood pressure, who works too hard, sleeps too little,
take stressful calls while driving a car littered with contraband from
McDonald's and Dairy Queen. An article about sleep apnea that I
printed out hidden at the bottom of the recycle bin—unread. Life vest
abandoned.

And then he materializes, oars
gently dip among the lily pads,
a Harris hawk swoops between us.
From across the water, his voice
carries …*there's my bride*.
He smiles and waves, unaware.
I am already practicing
my widow walk.

This is My Letter to the World
Based on Emily Dickinson's work by the same name

You, my fellows, now relieved of yet
another common face in the crowd
who was just trying to beat the light

when I was blindsided — by a bus,
or bullet, or gargantuan heartbreak
I didn't see coming—an event that

collapsed me in the middle of a city
street. A hush where there was once
a huge laugh and energy charged

with ions of regret. A sole decision
rued on a cellular level, for which
I could never be forgiven because,

dear global populace, I judged myself
on my intentions, while you, appropriately,
judged me on my actions. My fantasy

was to be remembered as a love-filled
soul in person form, but alas, my legacy
is an aspiring spirit who died in a swirl

of gut-level humanness. A paid first
responder paws through my keys, cough
drops, the first line of a poem inked on

the back of a Dollar Tree receipt, until
finding an ID with a photo from when
I was gray, before I started dying.

The Goldilocks Zone

*In astronomy, the Goldilocks Zone is **an area of space in which a planet is just
the right distance from its home star so that its surface is neither too hot nor too
cold.***

Her world a constant flux between
knowing she will never be enough
and apologizing that she is too much.
Seasons of walking through coastal
pines, always seeking a path of least
resistance, lesser of evils, best of
worst options. Too hot, too cold,

when rains wash away sand to expose
gnarled roots, pinecone littered trails.
Yet this November day, as she stands
at a point where trails branch before her,
something is different. For one split-second,
a divine moment, all is good.

Walking a carpet of dying pine needles,
each step releases a tangy, sweet scent.
Every inch of ground a shade of gold.
This will be fleeting, a text will come,
a call or email, which scrubs off the patina.
Things will quickly corrade.

But in this tableau, everything feels just right.
She listens to surf crash beyond the trees. Three
lovely hued paths at her feet. She cannot lose —
honey, amber, saffron.

Strawberry Moon

She always thought her life would have been better
had she been born in October in upstate New York,
sometime midmorning, when Carter was president.

She could have been named Mary Gold, like the
month's flower, or Autumn, teetering on the Libra
Scorpio cusp, balanced yet passionate. Arriving right

as the Concorde supersonic transport landed her maiden
flight into JFK. Her godmother would have decorated her
baptism party with terra cotta pots bursting mums,

the colors of caramels, sunflowers, fairy tale pumpkins.
She could have bounced into life, an acorn onto moss,
or a Honey Crisip apple cradled in a basket. But she cracked

open, an overripe watermelon in the deep southern sun,
a hundred plus miles north of Mexico where air is as hot
as Satan's breath. Her godmother strung up colored flowers

she crafted from tissue paper and handed out China Town
fans. She knew life would be hard for this child, a Cancer,
with the five-syllable first name and colic. Born breech

on an army base, into a battleground marriage, where
teenagers prepared for the jungles of Vietnam, at midnight
when the full moon burned like the end of a lit cigarette.

A *Frenemy* Blows up my Phone at the Sparkle Nail Salon

Through the glassed storefront, I see a quarter moon,
the opal tip of French manicure pointing at me
in accusation — each of your texts an attack because
I refuse to engage. This is not me cowering from
Courageous conversation, but knowing that once
you enter a power struggle, you have already lost.
I am a good friend, yet you continue to strain
the rope in a one-sided tug-of-war.

Don't mistake my *Good Nature* for vulnerability.
You invited a warrior to battle, my *Candy Apple Red*
nails grip a sword, polished toes work to maintain
balance and side-step your self-induced drama. In war,

I slay *Dragons*, but I will not acknowledge gaslighting,
your breath fiery as you tend your narrative, claws and
Fangs sharpened in excitement. I must save my colors
—mauves, pinks, dusty roses—for when real difficulties
Arise, to roll up my sleeves and come out swinging.

I am tempted to engage with a shimmery coat of
Bling It On but ask the manicurist for the smooth
orchid tones of *Power Moves*.

---

*Words in italics are nail polish names by ORY, Shynee Knobs, Lepo, M&N
Indie, PoisonedLacquer, OPI, & Essie*

COVID Quarantine Serenade

She came from a clan of psychological surgeons,
skilled emotional dissectors, quicker to amputate
a leg than mend a bone, comfortable with the sight
of blood. So she entered motherhood with scalpels,
retractors, clamps. Amazed by families where things
came easy, their first aid kits of fluffy cotton balls,
glow-in-the-dark Band-Aids.

Family never felt natural for her and her kids knew it.
Mom-dreams of singing "Frere Jacques" in rounds,
car bingo, turned into a silent minivan of headphones,
Nintendo. Game nights met with eyerolls, circled
into hours of TV. Sullen dinners, bickering vacations.
Each kid morphed from sacrificial lamb to turner
of the spit, and back.

Fueling fire, then extinguishing it. Aware they'd
leave needing what she could not give, she urged
them to go, build, be, something better than this.
Photos on her piano felt like an evidence board, faces
linked with imaginary red string, pushpins in a map,
periodic sightings, manhunts, obligatory holidays,
until March 15, 2020,

when they were mandated back home. She held her
breath for weeks as they marked territories to work,
study, Zoom, boundaries clear as crime scene tape.
But mid-April, a jigsaw puzzle appeared, meatless
Mondays began, then movie nights. As they built
with rediscovered Legos, new pathways formed
in their brains. In bunk beds

under ceiling stars she'd painted years ago, hearts
defrosted. Familial Frankenstein, they sutured together.
In June, before each returned to their own life, they
gathered at the piano to sing *Happy Birthday Dear
Mommy*, reluctant matriarch, armed with KN95s, hand
sanitizer. Her family, that stood six feet apart for decades,
a cohesive pod, unmasked.

Return Flight to BWI after Experiencing the Grand Canyon

A group of ravens are an unkindness, harbingers of death, inky scavengers. A tour guide says if I keep my eyes open, I'll see the nuisances everywhere. For me, Baltimore bred-and-buttered, Halloweens spent at Poe's grave, cheering on our beaked and taloned mascot, they bring delight. Not just big crows, but majestic. So as the masses photograph the literal wonder of the world, I shoots birds in a juniper tree. Some native tribes refer to ravens as psychopomps, connectors of spirits. When I was young and chose to change my life, I was told, "Don't believe in miracles? Stick around and be one!" They are everywhere: ebony fans over the Colorado, thick dashes in sagebrush, sparring atop a McDonald's dumpster. At night when the birds are no longer visible, I drive into Kaibab Forest, one of the pitch-blackest places in the country. I kill the car lights and walk under big sky. Above Ponderosa pine, each inch of heaven is showered with stars. Jupiter winks from the dusty sparkle of Milky Way, putting the day's grandness to shame. *Deep into that darkness.... dreaming dreams no mortal ever dared to dream before*, I leave the west with visions: stardust, raven, wind, varve of rust and violet, knowledge of a higher power's will for me, nothing else, nothing less, *nothing more.* As metallic wings fly me home to Charm City, I vow to connect my spirit to miracles large and small, crowd out fear and anger, avoid falling prey to my true nature.

A Man's Heart

They Crowned It Queen

T... ... ... a day in every homemaker's
life ... ... es to serve a dish that is
tri... ... otic ... arance, luxurious in flavor,
and ... ... eal in a ... t glowing color.

... occasion may come when the boss and
... wife come for their first meal, when the
famorous new neighbor is invited for lunch-
... ... when the new bridge club meets and the
girls come with their new finery, or a big
birthday or family celebration rolls around

The answer is the beautiful and delicious
Coronation chicken, which was crowned queen
of chicken dishes two months before Queen
Elizabeth dons the historic King Edward
crown in Westminster Abbey.

Its debut came when the Poultry and Egg
National Board served it to many of the
country's leading food editors at "Coronation
Chicken Day" ceremonies in New York.

Colorful as almost any dish can be, Corona-
... chicken consists of a half pineapple, hol-
... out and filled with a spicy chicken à la
... ture, topped with Parmesan cheese,
... a few minutes, and then surmounted
... ... "crown" made of an orange slice,
... shredded coconut.

Coronation Chicken

4 tablespoons butter, marg...
   fat
1 can (4-ounce) mushroom...
   or ⅓ pound fresh mushr...
⅓ cup flour
1 cup chicken broth or...
1 cup milk
1 teaspoon salt
1 teaspoon Worcestershi...
⅛ teaspoon pepper
⅛ teaspoon ground nu...
¼ cup (1½ ounces) sa...
¼ cup chopped green...
2 cups diced (½ to...
   chicken
3 pineapple shells
½ cup diced fresh p...
⅓ cup Parmesan ch...
   Paprika

Melt butter, marg...
mushrooms and br...
blend thoroughly. ...
chicken broth an...
stirring constantly...
thickened and co...
   Add salt, W...

Coronation Chicken

RECIPES

STATE JOURNAL
MARKET BASKET

Coronation Chicken Queen of New Dishes

Half Pineapple Is Filled with Creamed Fowl

By VIRGINIA BAIRD
(Journal Woman's Editor)

The other day the "trade" gathered in New York for a coronation chicken festival.

Everybody brought his or her best chicken recipe for competition.

Super flavors and aromas were tasted and savored. And the winner was really spectacular both in appearance and in delicious ingredients.

The Poultry and Egg National Board and the Northeastern Poultry Producers council... de... tailed instructions... the winner—coron... and the recipes fo... dishes. An aluminum... nt us the recipe... ered in the con... in totally ou... we received...

Coronation Chicken Is 'Something Different'

Phillips Stewart.

... cooks like to turn out fancy foods in their kitch-
...en serve them in some spectacular way. Regard-
...oronation chicken pictured is a spectacular dish.
... crown made from orange peel or the perky maraschino
...he top, the chicken is excellent.
...ou are looking for new flavors, try chicken with fresh
... Your guests will be intrigued.
... an added flavor, the chicken mixture is covered with Par-
...eese. If your family does not care for this bitey cheese,
...chicken mixture is a glorified chicken a la king and can
...with fresh cooked chicken or canned chicken.

Coronation Chicken.

(6 servings.)

...ablespoons butter or chicken fat
...-ounce can mushroom stems and pieces
...ablespoons flour
...p chicken broth or bouillon
...p rich milk
...poon salt
...f teaspoon Worcestershire sauce
...spoon pepper
...nutmeg

...icken Dishes

...ond nutmeg. Add almonds, green
...chicken and heat thoroughly. Ad
... Put chicken mixture in pin
...placed on a baking sheet; spr
...mesan cheese Place a piece o
...over the leaves to preve
...drying.
... Place in preheated br
...

...a whole pineapple dress fresh pineapple
one-half cup diced fresh pineapple
one-third cup grated Parmesan cheese
*2 large pineapples can be cut in three portions

...od:
... butter or chicken fat. Drain mushrooms and let simmer
... minutes. Stir in flour.
...ushroom liquid, chicken broth and milk., Cook, stirring
... until mixture is thickened. (Mixture should boil up
...s, almonds, sweet red pepper and chicken,
... in pineapple.
... in half or divide 2 large pineapples
... each piece. H

...rip
... and ... son whose ma
...Grand ... Frederic Coad will be an
...ay. June 13.
... The bride-elect is the d
... and Mrs. R

The Date: Summer, 1953.

The Occasion: The approaching coronation of Queen Elizabeth II.

The Setting: The remains of the British Empire, where commodities like sugar and meat were still subject to wartime rationing.

The coronation of Queen Elizabeth II was a great opportunity to relaunch Britain as a vibrant and colorful player in the world, after fifteen years of grim privation that began with the onset of the Second World War. A state luncheon for more than 300 foreign dignitaries marked the beginning of the celebration, and the nation's Minister of Works tasked Le Cordon Bleu cooking school in London to prepare and serve the food. The school had a student staff of well-trained British cooks, directed by event manager Constance Spry and the school's founder Rosemary Hume.

The signature dish for the feast was *Poulet Reine Elizabeth* (Queen Elizabeth's Chicken)—a chicken salad with one or two startling additions: a bright yellow creamy mayonnaise spiced with turmeric and curry powder, and a garnish of apricot puree. The chicken was added to the recipe pre-cooked (poached in a white wine stock, actually), as the dish was to be served cold for logistical reasons.

The recipe was published shortly afterwards, but by then it had gone viral—and like all viruses, it mutated to survive. People without turmeric or the ability to make crème fraîche made substitutions instead—which has led over the years to the kind of substandard chicken salad that disappointed the narrator in the poem *Coronation Chicken* in this book.

The recipes that follows are more authentic variants on the original post-war dish. The first comes direct from Le Cordon Bleu London, the school where the dish originated. The second, from *The Guardian* in 2011, taps ingredients uncommon sixty years earlier, and caters to a spicier and more modern palate.

SLIGHTLY ADJUSTED TRADITIONAL BRITISH CORONATION CHICKEN
SERVES 2

1 cooked chicken breast, finely diced
2 spring onions, finely sliced
2 g (half tsp) mild curry powder
2 g (half tsp) ground turmeric
60 g (2 oz) mayonnaise
1 tbsp crème fraîche (or whipped cream or Greek yoghurt)
1 tsp tomato ketchup
1 tbsp apricot nappage (sieved jam)
juice of 1 lime
small bunch coriander leaves
salt and pepper

Place the diced chicken and sliced spring onion into a large bowl.

Sprinkle curry powder and ground turmeric over them.

Add the mayonnaise, crème fraîche, tomato ketchup, apricot jam and lime juice. Stir to combine the mixture. Season with salt and pepper.

Roughly chop the coriander leaves. Add to the chicken mixture and stir to coat in the sauce. Then use the result as a sandwich filling or over rice.

21st CENTURY SPICIER VARIANT ON BRITISH CORONATION CHICKEN
SERVES 6

1.5 kg (3.5 pounds) chicken
1 cinnamon stick
5 black peppercorns
Pinch of saffron
1 tsp salt
4cm (1.5 inch) piece of fresh ginger
Bay leaf
5 tbsp good quality mango chutney
50g (1.5 ounces) dried apricots, finely chopped
2 tbsp good curry powder
2 tsp Worcestershire sauce
200ml (7 oz) mayonnaise
200ml (7 oz) Greek yoghurt
50g flaked almonds, toasted
Small bunch fresh coriander, chopped
Green salad and basmati rice, to serve

Put the chicken, breast-side up, in a large pan along with the cinnamon, peppercorns, saffron, salt, the bay leaf and half of the ginger and fill with cold water until only the top of the breast is exposed. Cover with a lid and bring to a simmer, then turn down the heat so only the occasional bubble rises to the surface. Cook gently for about one and a half hours until the juices run clear. Take out of the pan and set aside to cool, then remove the meat in bitc-sized pieces while lukewarm. Finely chop the rest of the ginger.

Put the mango chutney and apricots into a large bowl. Toast the curry powder in a dry frying pan until fragrant, then add the chopped ginger and stir both into the bowl, followed by the Worcestershire sauce, then the mayonnaise and yoghurt. Season to taste.

Once the chicken is cold, fold it through the dressing and refrigerate for at least a couple of hours before folding through most of the coriander and serving topped with the almonds, with a green salad and basmati rice.

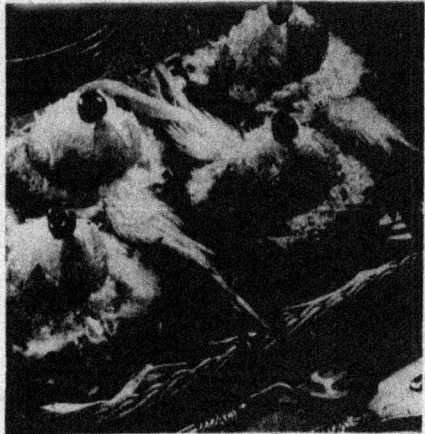

Coronation Chicken Is 'Something Different'

By Wilma Phillips Stewart.

Some cooks like to turn out fancy foods in their kitchens and then serve them in some spectacular way.

The coronation chicken pictured is a spectacular dish. Regardless of the crown made from orange peel or the perky maraschino cherry on the top, the chicken is excellent.

If you are looking for new flavors, try chicken with fresh pineapple. Your guests will be intrigued.

For an added flavor, the chicken mixture is covered with Parmesan cheese. If your family does not care for this bitey cheese, choose a mild American cheese.

The chicken mixture is a glorified chicken a la king and can be made with fresh cooked chicken or canned chicken.

Coronation Chicken.

(6 servings.)

4 tablespoons butter or chicken fat
1 4-ounce can mushroom stems and pieces
4 tablespoons flour
1 cup chicken broth or bouillon
1 cup rich milk
1 teaspoon salt
one-half teaspoon Worcestershire sauce
one-eighth teaspoon pepper
one-eighth teaspoon ground nutmeg
4 tablespoons chopped salted almonds
one-fourth cup chopped sweet red pepper
2 cups cooked diced chicken
3 whole pineapples*
one-half cup diced fresh pineapple
one-third cup grated Parmesan cheese

*2 large pineapples can be cut in thirds lengthwise

Coronation chicken is broiled in pineapple shells and decorated with crowns of orange peel.

From the Des Moines Register, Friday May 22nd, 1953

That would be all we need to write, except for the fact that a few months before the Coronation in 1953, the United States was gripped with coronation fever. To capitalize on this, and to promote the U.S. domestic poultry industry, the Poultry and Egg National Board sponsored a Coronation Chicken Day. This U.S. trade commission disseminated a recipe to any newspaper that cared to print it, containing such distinctly non-British ingredients as pineapple, and such arbitrary symbolism as a crown fashioned from orange peel.

This pretender to the throne, while it is technically the first dish to bear the name Coronation Chicken, doesn't merit a full recipe in a book like this, but it's easy enough to fabricate: Take half of a hollowed-out pineapple, fill it with Chicken à la King (a dish not named for royalty, but for the last name of a New York hotelier), and broil. Then top the whole thing off with an orange-slice crown, cocktail cherries, and shredded coconut.

Just don't do it around us.

Notes

"Praying with Mark Twain" contains quotes from Mark Twain (italicized).

"Homer's Warning to his Son" nods to Homer's The Odyssey.

"Mockingbirds" contains the first line and takes form from Ada Limón's "The Hurting Kind."

"A Nod to Robert Frost and Bill Wilson Off of Kamehameha Highway" contains quotes from Alcoholics Anonymous: The Story of How More Than One Hundred Men Have Recovered from Alcoholism by Bill W. and Robert Frost's poem "The Road Not Taken."

"Orbit of Venus de Milo's Marriage" nods to Alexandros of Antioch's statue Venus de Milo.

"Prayer of the Practical Mother" is borrowed from a traditional nursery rhyme, author unknow.

"Parable of the Prodigal Daughter" is based on the Gospel of Luke.

"Taking on Water" nods to Claude Monet's series Water Lilies, William Shakespeare's character Ophelia from Hamlet, and Virginia Woolf.

"Mother of the Bride: a Self-Portrait" nods to Mark Rothko's painting "Orange, Red, Yellow, 1961," Peter Paul Rubens, Jackson Pollock, and the song "Scarlet Begonias" written by Robert Hunter and performed by The Grateful Dead.

"Return Flight to BWI after Experiencing the Grand Canyon" quotes Edgar Allan Poe's "The Raven"

"Unforgiven," nods to Edgar Allan Poe and history of The Deer Park Tavern, Newark, DE

"And deliver us from evil" nods to the artwork of Frida Kahlo and a tribute to surrealist poet Alejandra Pizarnik

"Lucky Number" quotes lyrics from the musical Annie.

BIOGRAPHY

Maria Masington is a poet, author, and spoken word artist from Delaware. Her poetry has appeared in over two dozen publications including The News Journal, Rockvale Review, The Raven's Perch, The Broadkill Review, Never Forgotten: 100 Poets Remember 9/11, and by the University of Colorado. Seven of her short stories have been published in local and international presses.

Parnilis Media released Masington's first chapbook, *Mouth Like a Sailor*, in 2021. It was awarded first place by both the Delaware Press Association and National Federation of Press Women. She been acknowledged as a three-time Delaware Division of the Arts Fellow.

Maria is active in The Mad Poets Society and works as your friendly emcee to support the artistic community.

ALSO BY MARIA MASINGTON

Mouth Like a Sailor

Winner of the Delaware Press Association's and National Federation of Press Women's 2022 Award for Best Chapbook of Poetry.

Maria Masington's poetry is bold and unflinching, but at the same time warm and humane and humorous. She can be sentimental without being cloying, and direct without being harsh. In her world, Snow White attends AA. In her world, the everyday offers a peek into a much broader world, but remains grounded in reality and humor. This five-part collection of her poetry is salty and nautical in name only—it has a firm footing on solid ground.

Published by Parnilis Media, 63 pages, ISBN 978-1954895072